The Joy and Wonder of Christmas

The Joy and Wonder of Christmas

Steve Gannaway

Copyright © 2011 Steven K. Gannaway

All rights reserved. No part of this book may be used or reproduced in any manner whatsoever without written permission except in the case of brief quotations embedded in critical articles or book reviews.

ISBN: 978-0-9830047-1-4

The author may be contacted at
JoyAndWonder@TheMaineSeasons.com

The Maine Seasons
12 Lucerne St.
Springvale, ME 04083

Photos on cover and page 8 are by Mary Gillings Gannaway. The frontispiece drawing is by Kevin Donahoe.

"Mary" and "The Magi" were previously published in *Journeys*, but have been modified for use here. "The Shepherd Boy," "The Shepherd's Story," and "The Innkeeper," were expanded considerably from their card form and were also published in *Journeys*.

Dedication and Acknowledgments

This book is dedicated, first of all, to the memory of William F. Gannaway, my grandfather. By his example, he taught me all I have ever needed to know about living a life of love.

I thank my parents, Dick and Flo, and my siblings, Chris, Lynn, Jill, Scott and Susie, for the great Christmases I experienced growing up. Finally, I thank God for giving me Mary, Rick and Soriya, my wife and children. God created Christmas and still gives the best gifts of all.

Contents

Poems without a title are identified by first line.

Preface ix

The Christmas Card Poems
2011: The Infant in the Manger 3
2010: The Christmas Season 5

2009: Truth 7
2008: The Shepherd Boy 10
2007: Christmas Joy 13

2006: Snowflakes Dancing 15
2005: The Shepherd's Story 16
2004: What the Stable Mouse Saw 19

2003c: God's Son Is Born 21
2003: In the Manger an Infant Lies 22
2002: Stars Illumine the Winter Sky 23

2001: Snowflakes 24
2000c: In the Night 25
2000: It Was the Darkest Part Of Night 26

1999: As a Child in His Mother's Womb 28
1998: The Gentle Angel Choir Sings 29
1998: Trumpets Announce and People Cheer 30

1997: Christmas Gifts 32
1996: The Gift of Life 33
1994: Saplings Breathe the Morning Songs 34

1993:	Like a Hen that Proudly Rests	36
1991:	We Gather Together on Christmas Day	38
1990:	Late One Evening, I Sat Me Down	39
1989:	The Innkeeper	41
1987:	Though Once He Came	44
1986:	A Gift, a Gift	46
1985:	A Dust of Joy Upon the Ground	47
1983:	Once Shone a Star	48

More Joy and Wonder

A Star that Twinkles in the Sky	53
Baby's First Christmas	54
Beneath Their Ragged Cloaks They Sit	56
Christmas Morning	58
Cries and Groaning in the Night	60
In the Stillest Depth of Night	62
Christmas Days	64
Mary	65
Magi (Told by Balthazar)	71
PEACE	77
Christmas Questions	78
God Sent	80
Gifts: A Counter Cultural Christmas Card	81
The Tree He Would Never Forget	83
The Gift of Writing	97
Sharing the Joy and Wonder of Christmas	99

Preface

My first book, *Journeys*, was nearly five years in the making. It seemed like a very long time. It seems much less so when I consider that *The Joy and Wonder of Christmas* has been in-process for thirty years. In a mere nine months, a baby proceeds from conception to birth. This, however, is poetry, and sometimes poetry takes a little longer.

This volume was conceived in 1981, in North Dakota. As a Christmas gift for friends and family, I produced a mimeographed, eight-page collection of poems. I did the same in 1982. Most of the poems, though, had little connection to Christmas.

In 1983, I made my first Christmas card. Almost every year since then, I have created a new card, featuring an original Christmas poem. These twenty-eight Christmas card poems comprise the first part of *The Joy and Wonder of Christmas*.

Since they were previously placed before the public eye, albeit as cards, I wanted to refrain from further editing the poems and present them to you as published.

However, scattered among the poems were faults that might have shaken few other readers, but would have rattled my poetic sensibilities with earthquakes. To avoid having to recall to active service, the family's esteemed seismologist, Dick Maley, I took it upon myself to manipulate a few words or phrases along the fault lines.

Because Christmas is such a fertile subject for a poet and storyteller, I could not confine myself to poems for Christmas cards. Thus, *The Joy and Wonder of Christmas* has a second part, consisting of additional Christmas poems, a Christmas story, and a closing comment. More Joy and Wonder.

Yes, Christmas is a joyous and wondrous time. Families gather to share food, memories and gifts. Old friends get back in touch. We encounter a renewed spirit of generosity. This season of light and love affords us access to the joy and wonder of the first Christmas.

The previous paragraph portrays Christmas with buoyant optimism, but for some people, "It just ain't so." For them, Christmas is the season when memories become open sores. Christmas is filled with lonely battles against loss, pain, and depression.

My prayer for these sorrow-soaked souls is that the magnitude of the Christmas event will bring solace and healing. For, in the nativity, the Creator of the universe reached into our world with extraordinary humility. It was an act of deep and personal love.
Beginning with His birth in a stable, Jesus immersed Himself in the lives of the poor and the suffering, the hungry and the lost, the mourning and the alienated. In Hebrew, these are called, collectively, the anawim (an´ uh weem), the little ones of God. He opened His arms wide to embrace them, to embrace us, and to lift us to the heights of His heavenly throne.

May the hope-infused poems of this volume reflect the joy of Jesus' birth to all of God's children. And, may the anawim stand open-mouthed in wonder that the King of Glory came for them.

Regardless of the season that finds you reading this book, I hope that it pulls aside the veils of your memory. Perhaps a particular image will flash into your mind, a recollection of being touched by the joy and wonder of Christmas.

If this should happen, take time to sit back and savor that memory. Don't rush to the next poem—it isn't going anywhere. Life would likely permit you the luxury of letting the joy and wonder of Christmas wash over you once more. Take advantage of the opportunity.

May the joy and wonder of Christmas be ever in your heart.

The Christmas Card Poems

The Infant in the Manger (2011)

With winter swirling in the night,
She was a sentry standing guard,
Alertly scanning flakes of white
For paired bright beams in her front yard.

Some hours before, Dad brushed the car;
Strong winds, though, dumped the snow right back.
"The clinic is not very far,"
Said Mom, as she picked up her pack.

"Some angels helped at Jesus' birth,
While others sang up in the sky.
Pray now that angels come to earth
And bring me help from God on high."

The girl did pray all Christmas Eve,
For Mom and for the baby, too,
Damp prayers in her pajama sleeve.
Then two lights flashed; her watch was through.

With boots and coat both left behind,
She staggered through the thigh-high snow.
The howling wind, she did not mind;
With Mom home safe, just let it blow.

The trio, dried off, wrapped up, warm,
Thanked God for infants safely born,
Divine protection in the storm,
And Jesus' birth on Christmas morn.

Her mom had Baby's photograph;
It showed an infant, wrinkled, brown.
She seized it, bounding like a calf;
They smiled at where she put it down.

For weeks the manger had been bare
In the crèche beneath the tree,
But now the photograph was there
To spark the sacred memory.

The Christmas Season (2010)

Why do shoppers fuss and hurry?
Like so many ants, we scurry.
      What present could we buy and share
      As precious as the gift conferred
      Through a young girl in a stable where
      Her Baby's birth that night occurred?

All primed to make a good display,
While school and work give way to play.
      No mere party joined that night
      The outcast shepherds from the slope,
      With wealthy men who trailed star's light,
      And heaven's heralds of new hope.

Our patience dims as lights are strung
And shiny ornaments are hung.
> His nursery in a stable brought
> Scant comfort for the Little Boy,
> But starlight by the cave was caught
> And bathed them all with simple joy.

The Christmas season is so busy,
That it leaves us feeling dizzy.
> Give Christmas back simplicity,
> Each piece put in its proper place.
> Regain the true felicity
> Found gazing on the Infant's face.

Truth (2009)

The full moon with unblinking eye,
While looking from the cloudless sky,
Thinks it sees a snowman there,
Wrapped in woolly winter wear.
But truth may differ in its hue,

As with the boughs now thick with snow,
Where Moon must deeply look to know
This is no snowman but a tree
That in the summer green will be.
The truth fears not to look anew.

Though precious is each babe conceived,
Some folks, by vision, are deceived.
Once in a cave, on hard-packed earth,
A youthful Jewish girl gave birth.
When all else fails, the Truth breaks through.

By normal sight, like any child;
A healthy boy, in spirit, mild.
But those who gazed with knowing eyes
Perceived the Newborn otherwise.
The truth may be profoundly new.

An Infant born in poverty,
But heir to highest majesty.
This season celebrates God's Gift,
Who came to make the darkness lift,
Who gives the means to know the true.

Discern the truth and then be awed
At how each person mirrors God.
Receive this priceless gift anew
And let your eyes more truly view
The gift and glory that are you.

The Shepherd Boy (2008)

Children to the shepherd went
Excitedly to make their plea,
Would he one more time consent
To tell them of that wondrous night?
He closed his eyes and memory
Flowed like this before his sight.

Young Jacob to the hills was sent
To tend his father's sheep.
Like other shepherds, with no tent,
He learned that lying on the ground
At the sheepfold gate to sleep,
He would hear if threats came 'round.

Thus, the night that angels came,
Jacob lay in bright starlight
That flickered in the sky like flame.
He heard the trumpet blasts resound,
Announcing choirs left and right,
Taking stations all around.
The other shepherds, too, awoke
As angelic anthems filled the night.
Then one angel neared and spoke,

"Do not fear, we bring to you
News of joy for Israel
That her wait at last is through.

The Messiah, born this night,
With humanity will dwell,
That it with God may reunite."

Running like it was a race,
In the blink of an angel's eye,
Jacob came upon the place.
The shepherd boy, as he drew near,
Slowed, becoming suddenly shy;
What if they did not want him here?

Then the parents stepped aside
And at the manger made some room,
So he approached, eyes open wide.
There he saw upon the straw,
Like a light dispelling gloom,
The Child who filled his heart with awe.

When Jacob knelt, the Infant raised
A tiny wrinkled hand.
The shepherd boy looked on, amazed,
Then placed his finger in the palm,
And though he did not understand,
His pounding heart grew quiet, calm.

Babies are blind when born, he knew,
Yet, from the manger, those dark eyes
Caught his own and saw right through.
Minutes like a moment passed
And then he rose with stifled sighs,
Making way for those less fast.

They, within the small cave massing,
Before the rough-hewn manger knelt
As rising sun marked night's swift passing.
Returning to flocks up on the hill,
The shepherd boy within him felt
The Newborn's touch and presence still.

Jacob was more than satisfied,
While time slipped by from year to year,
To watch the sheep on this hill side.
Then heaven on the shepherd smiled:
He saw the Teacher drawing near,
And recognized in Him, the Child.

He had to follow, could not stay,
But, that will have to be, I fear,
A tale to tell another day.

Christmas Joy (2007)

Can you hear the angel calling east and west,
Heralding the birth of the King of Kings?
Ranks of seraphs appear, hundreds abreast;
Inviting shepherds each one of whom brings
Small wooden carvings of dog, sheep or hare,
Toys to amuse the Child, their Lord.
Many miles removed from there,
A group still follows the star that soared,
Summoning all of us to join them where

Jesus is born, first in stable, then in hearts,
Only true Son of the Father,
Yet now and ever both savior and brother.

Snowflakes Dancing (2006)

Christmas joy comes from the sky:
Snowflakes dancing as they fly,
Sometimes crystals, small and tight—
Large and fluffy ones tonight;
Like a pillow filled with down,
They give comfort without sound.

Eastern skies were not aglow,
Rooster, still, had yet to crow,
But already children stared
At the tree and gifts prepared.
So began this joyful day,
Filled with laughter, food and play.

Near forgotten, but not quite,
Was the moment on the night
God revealed His face on earth
Through the Christ child's humble birth,
Letting us see partially
Through the veil of mystery.

At day's end, as snowflakes fall,
Silence helps us to recall
Blessings that have come our way,
Leading us, perhaps, to say,
From this peace-filled interlude,
Words to show our gratitude.

The Shepherd's Story (2005)

Come my friend, please have a seat,
And hear the tale I have to tell
Of how The One I came to meet.

It seemed an ordinary night,
Though there was a certain star
That shown uncommonly bright.

Calmness passed among the sheep
As they settled in small groups
And soon were drifting off to sleep.

We shepherds, too, had settled down
To a night of quiet listening
As we reclined upon the ground.

Then suddenly arose a gale
That swept the ordinary
From every hill and sheltered vale.

From drowsiness and slumber,
We and our sheep were snatched,
And filled instead with wonder.

For in the great wind's wake
Came music most profound
Such that only angels make.

We bowed before the blinding light
Of the gathered heavenly chorus,
Each singing seraph shining bright.

Then from their midst one angel spoke
About the long awaited birth
Of our Messiah and our Hope.

It filled our hearts to the very brim
That for shepherds he had sent—
And asked that we attend him.

So urging ahead our sheep
We followed as the angels led
With never a thought of sleep.

On into Bethlehem Town
And behind the largest inn,
Where we a common stable found

And, there, a most uncommon child.
Awake, he lay within the manger
Where a mound of straw was piled.

We gazed upon the infant small
With wonder and amazement
That he had come to save us all.

So we bowed to him, our Lord,
And more precious than purest gold,
Into his hands, our hearts we poured.

Though shepherds did we remain,
This night of holy wonder
Had left none of us the same.

What the Stable Mouse Saw (2004)

Long ago in a distant place
A stable was carved in a hillside bare.
Several donkeys shared this space,
Jostling for spots at the manger there.

In the back, 'neath a pile of stones,
A small gray mouse had made his nest.
He scurried about trying to pad his bones,
With scant success on his tireless quest.

On an evening when stars shone bright
Some strangers to the stable came.
"What poor folks must these two be,
With little for themselves and none for me,"
Muttered the small gray watcher to the night,
But he slipped on closer just the same.

From her beast, the woman slid down,
Gently helped by the walk-weary man.
She lay upon the straw-strewn ground
And a night of silent watching began.

When were ended her hours of toil,
The woman was rewarded with a precious prize—
A boy was born with demeanor royal,
The very Word of God in human guise.

The mouse then heard a wonderful thing
As angels filled the stable, filled the air,
With music like none ever heard before,
While shepherds to the stable's door
Flocked like sheep to hear them sing
And see the Infant lying there.

Still more marvels the mouse did see
As, days later, to the stable rode
Wealthy men, in number three,
With spices sweet and yellow gold.

Soon thereafter, the blessed pair,
Bundling the Child with greatest care,
Left the stable and watcher there
Who this wonder was allowed to share.

God's Son Is Born (2003, cover)

God's Son is born
      into a world

Where swords are drawn
      and spears are hurled.

He comes to bring
      us peace of heart

That we, His hands,
      might peace impart.

In the Manger, an Infant Lies (2003)

In the manger, an infant lies,
Addressing the world with piercing cries
That resound from the stable far,
Igniting, in the sky, a star
Whose light, reflecting off the wing
Of each angel there to sing,
Leads poor shepherds beneath the trees
To honor the Child on bended knees.

For, in that simple, humble place,
They gazed upon the very face
Of the newborn Prince of Peace
Whose touch makes fear and hatred cease.
He was born into a world
Where guns are drawn and missiles hurled—
He came to cause a change of heart,
That we, His hands, might peace impart.

Stars Illumine the Winter Sky (2002)

Stars illumine the winter sky
And silently remind us why
We hold this night in such esteem.
Images come as in a dream...

In a stable, man and wife,
Are watchful of the precious life
Of He who in the manger lies,
Who pierces night with newborn cries.

Soon come shepherds, timid and shy,
Joined by angels who fill the sky
With heav'nly melodies and laud
To a loving, gracious God.

They celebrate with song this birth:
God's Son, God's gift, upon the earth.
So, let the sky with starlight bright
Remind us all, "Rejoice this night!"

Snowflakes (2001)

Heavy white clouds with bounty bulge,
The glory of God's love divulge
As they countless flakes release,
Bright as stars and soft as fleece.

Every falling flake unique
Like each child with arms upraised
Catching crystals with hand and cheek,
Eyes wide open and amazed.

Sign and symbol of God's grace
Are falling snow and smiling face,
But most of all is Jesus' birth:
The gift of God to all the earth.

In the Night (2000, cover)

In the night,
      to shepherds came
Angels, wondrous
      news to proclaim:
"Born this night is
      the Promised One,
The Messiah,
      God's own Son."
      Luke 2: 8-12

It Was the Darkest Part of Night (2000)

It was the darkest part of night,
With but a star providing light
And silence broken just by sheep
Stirring gently in their sleep
While night caressed their curly fleece
With lightly scented balm of peace.

Shepherds at watch began to doze
Until the sound around them rose
Of voices spiraling in song,
Which gentle breezes bore along
To righteous hearts upon the earth
About the Christ Child's wondrous birth.

Responding to the song they heard
And to the angels' joyful word,
The shepherds left their flocks alone.
And turned to where the star now shone.
Anxiously they hurried along,
Accompanied by angel-song.

Behind an inn, they climbed a slope
With hearts that pounded in the hope
That before them they would find
The savior of all humankind
Whom the prophets contemplated:
The Messiah long awaited.

They found at last a Child asleep
Within a cave 'mid shadows deep,
Cast by a torch hung on the wall.
Neither king in his royal hall
Nor wealthy noble did they find,
But a carpenter, strong and kind.

A simple man stood with his wife
Gazing down at the Gift of Life
With eyes that filled with tears of love
As angel voices sang above
While the shepherds flocked around
To marvel at the Child they'd found.

For in their hearts, all gathered there
Saw in the crib a gift most rare:
A child Who, when His manhood gained,
Would spread His arms for captives chained,
Who, with His words and touch, would heal,
And, with His life, heaven's gate unseal.

While Sheltered In His Mother's Womb (1999)

While sheltered in his mother's womb,
He journeyed south to Bethlehem;
Safe within His warm, dark room,
His mother's love protected Him.
As each day, they closer came
To the appointed time of birth,
He longed to leave that loving frame
And show His face upon the earth.

Already drained, a sorry sight,
Joseph, Mary, and unborn child
Could find scant pity for their plight
While from inn to inn they filed.
Thus, Jesus put His Godly might
Aside and in a simple cave was born,
Angelic voices filled the night,
Accompanied by harp and horn.

He bore within a secret flame
That sought to help, to heal each child
Of the Father from Whom He came.
The hurt, the lost, and the reviled,
In whose cause He freely came,
That they, with God, be reconciled
And in His peace would shed their shame
And know themselves His beloved child.

The Gentle Angel Choir Sings (1998c)

The gentle angel
      choir sings
As is born
      the King of Kings.

Trumpets Announce and People Cheer (1998)

Trumpets announce and people cheer
As the mighty king draws near.
In silken garb is he arrayed
While his royal retainers parade.

Accompanied by such display
Are earthly rulers along their way;
But not like this, the King of Kings.
To darkest silent night He brings

Gentle angel choirs to sing,
A star to light the gathering
Around the manger where He lay
Upon a meager bed of hay.

Not like other kings was He,
Born to life in luxury.
He came to touch, to soothe, to heal,
The sin and pain from which we reel.

Thus the Prince of Peace was born,
Who, to the weary and heart-worn,
Has brought His gift of healing love;
To us has brought His healing love.

Christmas Gifts (1997)

The snowflakes falling from the sky
Remind us of the One on high
Whose gifts envelope us each day
As snow now blankets children's play.

We sometimes take these gifts in stride,
Or think we earn them and take pride,
Or ignore them altogether
As birds regard a fallen feather.

Remember now the Christmas love
Poured freely out by God above:
His Son, as pure as falling snow,
A gift for all who stand below.

Let all who see the snow drift down,
Hear children raise a joyful sound,
Or know the healing touch of love,
Give thanks this day to God above.

The Gift of Life (1996)

Gifts are given on Christmas Day,
Models to build and games to play,
But compared to this all else is thorn:
The gift of life, a girl is born.

Colored wrappings light the eyes,
Some gifts expected, some surprise,
but what bestows a greater joy?
The gift of life, a baby boy.

Clothing, toys, and memories,
Beneath countless Christmas trees,
Better than these to be obtained:
The gift of life and health regained.

Gifts exchanged in heart-felt love,
Yet none exceed that from above
When early that first Christmas morn,
The Gift of Life, the Lord, was born.

Saplings Breathe the Morning Songs (1994)

Saplings breathe the morning songs;
For the wind, each young branch longs;
Adults stretch out to their full height,
Day by day and night by night,
To cast their voices on the breeze
In sweetly scented melodies.

In deepest cold, they start to sing;
Fresh, fragrant tunes are sung in spring;
Warm refrains summer breezes bring.
But, as fall songs to winter flow,
The pines take on a special glow,
And in their gentle harmonies
Their song evokes bright memories
Of angel-song above the trees.

Angels sang for joy that night,
At Jesus' birth before their sight.
The trees now sing in mem'ry of
That gift of joy, that gift of love,
Which coming from the Holy Birth
Flows like the wind to all the earth.

Like a Hen that Proudly Rests (1993)

Like a hen that proudly rests
'Pon precious eggs within her nest,
So the tree stands glittering o'er
Presents stacked upon the floor.

It flashes lights to catch our eye
And coyly will not tell us why.
But when we all have gathered round,
It breathes contentment with no sound.

For some it may have been awhile
Since last we touched or shared a smile
Because of distance, miles or pain,
But here we are together again.

Perhaps the star that shown so bright
In the Holy Land that night
Has sent her children to our tree
To call us all to harmony.

And in that harmony to know
The One whose birth the great star's glow
Set as a beacon shining bright
To beckon shepherds in the night.

Recall His birth and why He came;
His love for us remains the same.
Like lights still twinkling on the tree,
His love is calling you and me.

We Gather Together on Christmas Day (1991)

We gather together on Christmas day,
Arms extended and bearing love.
Carols of joy we sing and play
With choirs of angels from above.

Packages wrapped in colors bright
Remind us of a special night
When a child was born, dark and small,
While candles flickered on the wall.

There's angel music in our mind
As sheep and shepherds come to find
The newborn Child, God's gift to all,
Snuggly wrapped in His mother's shawl.

We gather together on Christmas day
To celebrate the royal birth.
We join the angels as they pray
For goodwill to all, peace on earth.

Late One Evening I Sat Me Down (1990)

Late one evening, I sat me down,
Bones and muscle in a weary mound,
And watched in silence as snowflakes fell.
The drifting flakes, large and white,
Were whispering softly, doves in flight
Rising, startled by a lone church bell.

I listened to the fluttering sound
As they swirled and danced above the ground
'Til whispering wings became a voice
That spoke of birth beneath a star,
The men and women from near and far
Who in the babe found cause to rejoice.

Not doves, but words, swirled in the night.
"Peace" came close while "hunger" took flight;
"Justice" advanced as away "fear" flew.
My head jerked up, eyes open wide,
My dream a treasure held inside...
But is that not a dove's soft coo?

The Innkeeper (1989)

Short and stout with white whiskers long
That hid his face, except his eyes,
Which ever gleamed, as if to song,

His voice was deep and laughter flowed
Like a torrent from deep within
That flooded hearts before it slowed.

This man, the keeper of the inn,
The dark traveler's knock acknowledged
And weary plea heard with chagrin.

"No, no, there is no room within.
The beds are full, the floors as well.
I fear that you must leave, my friend."

But to the tale extended ear
As the traveler pleaded more
And spoke about the birth so near.

He could not send the pair away.
"Behind the inn, a stable lies.
You will find it along that way."

So, following his outstretched arm,
In the stable they sought shelter
From bandits, cold, and other harm.

The keeper of the inn, that night,
From his sleep by cries was wakened,
And saw the sky with stars alight.

To the window, he ran to gaze
On the scene around his stable:
The milling sheep beneath star-blaze,

Horses, cattle, and shepherds, too,
Who told him of the choir's song
And the child they had come to view.

He felt the wonder that held the throng
And his heart poured out with laughter long
That harmonized with angelic song.

We hope that you, too, this wonder know,
And pray this Christmas season that
Your heart with joy may overflow.

Though Once He Came (1987)

Behold
>He comes,
>>A glowing star,
Growing bright
>To banish night.

Though once He came
>As infants come,
Crying blindly
>Throughout the night,
Beneath the stars
>That flicker and fade,
Within a cave
>Darkly watching—
Behold,
>He comes,
>>A glowing star
Growing bright,
>To banish night.

Though once a youth,
>Living, breathing;
Against the pain,
>Silent, seething,
Until, a man,
>He dared to speak,
And more than man

Behold,
> He comes,
>> A glowing star
Growing bright,
> To banish night.

And now the day
> May shortly come
When, in a world
> That quakes with fear,
A sound that, like
> Hooves thund'ring rolls—
And horn and shout
> To hearken all:

Behold,
> He comes,
>> A glowing star
Growing bright,
> to banish night.

A Gift, a Gift (1986)

 A gift, a gift:
        A child is born!
Let joyful rain
        And rainbows arched
Upon our cheeks
        The earth renew.

Again, again,
        A child is born,
And with each one
        Is hope reborn—
For much as this
        The Christ Child came.

Anointed, too,
        Is she, is he,
To be our hope,
        To bring us life,
To heal our hearts
        That we might feel
And know that love
        Is, too, a gift.

A gift, a gift;
        A child is born!

A Dust of Joy Upon the Ground (1985)

A dust of joy upon the ground,
Falling there with scarce a sound.
As palms would one day on the street
He and donkey greenly greet,
So the snow falls Christmas day,
And in the silence seems to say:
"Remember Him whose birth, this day,
You celebrate with joyful play,
Eating, drinking, giving gifts,
Lifting hearts and healing rifts."

A dust of joy upon the ground,
Falling there with scarce a sound.
Jesus born beneath the star
After parents had traveled far.
Music drifted from the sky;
The earth gave forth a whispered sigh.
A promise given, gift bestowed:
Love and joy, the seeds He sowed,
And peace to all of those who know
He speaks to them in falling snow.

Once Shone a Star (1983)

Once shone a star
      a twinkling light
That drew the three
      on journey far
To see the One,
      to heed His call;
A signal light
      that blazed for all:
Women who hate
      and men who fear
All who differ
      in looks or views.

A star once pierced
      a hate-hued sky
To bring us all
      a happy word;
Silent beacon
      surrounded by
A music deep
      in brassy tones
That rang profound
      in words of peace.

Strangers, neighbors,
    shepherds, and kings,
Now called as one
    to gather round
The One whose birth
    might bring about
A hope for peace
    and dignity
For the children,
    both theirs and ours.

More Joy and Wonder

A Star Twinkles in the Sky

A star that twinkles in the sky,
"The Lord is come," its piercing cry.
Angels approach, awash in song;
The shepherds follow right behind.
The trekking magi won't be long,
Let's go and see what they shall find:
A star that twinkles in the sky,
"The Lord is come," its piercing cry.

Baby's First Christmas

Her little eyes were frozen by
Each colored twinkling light
That, on the tree, from low to high,
Were placed for her delight.

In the months that followed birth
Such wonders she had seen—
To comfort her and bring her mirth,
As if she was a queen.

But none like this was there before;
What glory and surprise!
Yet, it seemed, there was still more
To catch and hold her eyes.

On the big tree's lowest bough,
Just there, a white light shone;
It did not twinkle then and now,
And hung there all alone.

Beneath the light, a stable stood,
And scattered figures, too,
Plain and simple like the wood,
But sparkling like the dew.

\\

She could not know, not yet at least,
The meaning of the scene,
Or why it led to such a feast,
The like she had not seen,

It is the infant, carved and small,
That shows the reason why.
God's Son, with arms outstretched for all,
For us would later die.

As years went by, she did forget
So much of this first year,
But in her thoughts this scene glows yet,
And fills her heart with cheer.

Beneath Their Ragged Cloaks They Sit

Beneath their ragged cloaks they sit
Upon the hillside with their sheep
Taking turns with welcome sleep.

When one of them observes a star
That blazes in the cloudless sky,
He asks aloud, "I wonder why."

No answer from his fellows comes,
But from the sky there is a sound
Of music swirling all around.

He glances skyward fearfully,
And wakes his friends that they might hear
The voices coming still more near.

They sing of joy, they sing of birth,
They sing to shepherds on the earth
And call them to a hallowed place.

Afraid to go, afraid to stay,
The shepherds slowly make their way
Along the path the voices lead.

Up to a cave by torches lit
The shepherds stumble, bit by bit,
And there they find a sleeping child...

And there they find a greater Light
Than any star, however bright,
And humbly bow before their Lord.

Christmas Morning

A pair of parents, children, two--
An early morning in the car
That finds each eager, seeking You
In a place they know You are.

They slowly pull into the lot,
Then, like those seekers from afar,
Who left their homes with just one thought,
Approach the door beneath the star.

As "Silent Night" intones the choir
They pull the door and step inside,
Where all is lit, ablaze like fire,
And to its source on currents ride:

A half-formed hut awash with hay
With figures molded from the earth;
For this they've come at break of day,
An image of Your humble birth.

Before the figures, bow, then kneel,
Pour out their hearts, but not to clay—
It cannot waken what they feel,
But, like a finger, points the way.

Filled seats this simple scene surround
And as they rise to seek a place
The front row dwellers shift around
To make for them sufficient space

That they might join those gathered there,
Where wondrous words and joyous song
Recall that gift beyond compare,
The Savior's birth, awaited long.

The service lasts an hour, more,
But they ignore the watch and clock,
For being there is not a chore--
They find great joy within Your flock.

The time arrives for them to leave
And this they do with equal joy--
The children trying to believe
Their tree now shields that much sought toy.

But in their hearts, the children know
That of their gifts, the greatest one
Just God, from heaven could bestow--
And You were born, the Father's Son.

Now, home to gifts and meal prepared
For neighbors, friends and family,
And with the stranger also shared—
Your birth gave hope, and so must we.

Cries and Groaning In the Night

Cries and groaning in the night,
Beneath a star that burns most bright
Until a final cry is heard,
Virginal, before a word
Of wonder at the sight is spoken
Or seals on gifts are slit or broken.

Joy for Joseph and for Mary;
Shepherds in the foreground tarry;
Music drifts upon the breeze;
A golden glow is all one sees.

A baby born like many others,
As children of so many mothers.
Yet, to those who gather round,
Something more is to be found
In this Child born in the night
And sleeping now before their sight.

What it is, not all can say,
As the night slides into day,
But something whispers in the heart
And none is eager to depart
From the child who holds them here,
Whose presence frees their minds from fear.
Why this is they do not know,
Only that for them it's so.

Thus the picture formed for us
Of the birth of Christ Jesus;
Our voices echo with the joy
At the birth of one small boy,
Though we know the joy is marred
By hammer wielded by a guard,
And by spear sunk in the side
Of Jesus after He had died.

Still, our hearts affirm as true
What we watch from angels' view.
A day of joy and great delight,
For this Child born in the night
Will the world, at last, transform.
Let joy on earth become the norm.

In the Stillest Depth of Night

In the stillest depth of night,
Above a silent sleeping town,
The sky shone like a royal crown,
Ablaze with myriad diamonds bright.

In their midst, a star so great
It dwarfed the others in the sky.
It caught a shepherd's weary eye
And made him tremble for his fate.

For surely, thought this lonely man,
The star, an omen bore for him,
And signs like this are often grim
For those who labor on the land.

Watching over dozing sheep,
He pondered matters curved and straight
Diversely meeting mean and great
When his thoughts sank into sleep.

He woke to music sweet and clear
That bore his heart to heaven's door,
That place where angel voices soar
And washed away his former fear.

They called him to a stable dim
Where other shepherds stood in awe.
For more than just a child they saw,
But the very Son of Him

Who formed the earth, and man from clay,
Who called His own from slavery
Thus ending their captivity.
For, so he heard the angels say.

He bowed his head, felt teardrops fall
And knew that life could hold no fear
For one whom Glory had drawn near,
Who had received the angels call.

The star's bright light would turn to shade.
The angels' song would drift away,
But in their hearts would ever stay
The Love of God which would not fade.

"You who watch over sheep by night,
Know that My love for you is great.
I lead you to salvation's gate;
My newborn Son will be your light."

Christmas Days

Christmas days recalled when gifts
Flowed from the sparkling tree
Like lava, honey of the earth,
Pouring forth in crimson and gold.

Christmas days recalled with hand
Upon the arm: eleven-fifteen.
Sleep walking to the midnight Mass,
Where we sang with joy unbounded.

Christmas days recalled when snow
Skipped and danced down to the ground,
A special delivery gift God sent,
Delighting close-cropped little boys.

Christmas days recalled with love
Rising as steam from turkey breasts,
That we inhaled, savored, and passed
For all to take and taste.

Mary

Just fourteen was Mary then,
Pledged to Joseph, a carpenter;
She sewed at the window when
God sent to her a messenger.

As Mary worked, she could not know,
An angel was to visit,
But breeze outside began to blow,
Becoming something exquisite.

Gabriel, glowing like the sun,
Told her God had favored her
And chosen her to bear His Son.
She felt, not doubt, but wonder stir.

She asked how such a thing could be
And he explained, God's Spirit could
Pass over her as soundlessly
As shadows of her mother would.

"The Child that would be born to you
Would be holy, God's own Son."
She said, "I am God's servant true,
So, as you say, let it be done."

Gabriel added one thing more,
That, barren and advanced in years,
Her cousin conceived six months before;
Mary's joy flowed in streams of tears.

Though strongly encouraged to stay,
Mary was patiently insistent.
She was needed without delay,
Though her cousin's home was distant.

Elizabeth cried out with joy
When Mary came into her view;
Her soon-to-be-born little boy
Leapt in joyful greeting, too.

Three months, she helped Elizabeth,
Until after John was born.
She then returned to Nazareth,
Arriving weary and foot-worn.

Her pregnancy was clear to see
And hurtful stories started spreading.
Joseph, gently and quietly,
Made plans to stop the wedding.

But Gabriel came to him by night
And spoke within a dream,
"You worry over Mary's plight,
But God is acting to redeem."

The angel went on, "Mary bears
The Son of God inside her womb,
You may marry her without these cares.
In heart and home now make her room.

An edict issued from Caesar's hand
Compelled each leader to conduct a count
By each family group or band,
To determine their tax amount.

Since Joseph was of David's line,
To Bethlehem they had to go,
But paths at times were serpentine,
And hilly roads made travel slow.

Joseph walked the donkey Mary rode,
Nazareth, Samaria, and on,
Mary shared his pain as Joseph strode
From dawn until sun's light was gone.

Her child had grown week by week;
Now, day by day, discomfort grew,
But no complaint did Mary speak,
Though Joseph watched her face and knew.

Through Bethany and five miles more,
At last the town of Bethlehem.
It was day's end and she was sore,
So, Joseph sought a place for them.

He checked each inn they passed in town.
Said many keepers of an inn,
"Although I hate to turn you down,
 I have not any room within."

One continued, "I am afraid,
There is no space on bed or floor—
Like sheathes they are arrayed,
Tightly packed, no room for more."

An innkeeper at last they found
Who, though he had for them no space,
Added as they turned around,
"Behind the inn, a sheltered place,

A stable, if you wish to check..."
"We thank you, sir," said Joseph sighing.
Her arms around the donkey's neck,
Mary waited, softly crying.

Behind the inn they sought the stable
And found a cave dug in the hill,
A hay-filled manger, small wood table,
And five donkeys, quiet and still.

Beyond the reach of bright star light,
Joseph made a bed of hay.
Uncomfortably, deep in the night,
Awake and praying, Mary lay.

He gently wiped her face to soothe her,
Then Joseph sat nearby to wait;
He soon fell deeply into slumber;
His exhaustion was so great.

The time arrived, but brought no fear,
As Mary did what must be done.
She did not see the angels near,
Until with joy she held her son.

A little later from outside,
She heard the rustling sound of feet;
She stood, with Joseph at her side,
And greeted shepherds with their sheep.

Nervous, respectful, and eager,
And not knowing what to say,
The shepherds slowly approached her
And saw the manger where He lay.

When they found they were not spurned
The shepherds gladly told their tale:
From glorious angels they had learned
That God had reached out through the veil.

These men, like all in Israel,
Awaited God's Anointed One;
Now, joy like rain from heaven fell,
For they had found Him in her Son.

Surprises came from every side,
The shepherds' tale was but the start,
And Mary kept these things inside
To ponder often in her heart.

The Magi (Told by Balthazar)

Though some have called us sages,
We merely read the skies
That mutely gaze upon us
With wisdom in their eyes.

Exploring heaven's insight,
We saw the royal star
Proclaim a king of unmatched might
A monarch from afar.

It was a bit confusing;
The message was not clear.
It seemed that He was reigning,
And yet His birth was near.

The star was not to be ignored.
Yes, we stargazers three
Were called to meet this mighty lord,
And see His majesty.

Aware the journey could be long
And brigands think us prey,
We formed a party fifty strong
And soon got underway.

As dogs, while hunting in a band,
Pursue without a rest,
We, day by day and land by land,
From Persia traveled west.

We tracked the star, a beacon,
Ablaze up in the sky,
But near the River Jordan
It ceased to shine on high.

With Jordan River just behind,
We asked in Jericho,
And they were of a single mind,
"In New Shalom, they'll know."

Our guide no longer lit the skies,
So we proceeded there,
And found a city of good size
With bustle everywhere.

We went before the one who reigned,
King Herod was his name.
He listened, but his face grew pained
On hearing why we came.

The king found in Jerusalem
This answer from the scribes:
"It is the town of Bethlehem
The prophet here describes."

But Herod ordered us to wait,
Then summoned us by night
With urgent questions on the date
The star revealed its light.

If God's Messiah could be found,
The king intended to
Bestow his gift, make trumpets sound
With welcome from each Jew.

"So, when you find God's Holy One,"
Come back and please tell me,"
His voice was warm as morning sun
Which led us to agree.

When Herod said that we could go,
We did not wait for day,
But hurried as the welcome glow
Of starlight showed the way.

It showered light upon the place,
A watch-fire for our sake.
Our party labored at the pace
And fell back in our wake.

A strangely busy town, we found,
And filled with sheep, a horde,
Through which in haste we quickly wound,
By shepherds quite ignored.

We neared a cave carved in a hill;
Had heaven missed its aim?
Or was it true and did it still
His royal birth proclaim?

Remaining distant, yet we saw
The Babe for whom we came,
Within a trough with little straw
To cushion His small frame.

Recalling who the Infant was,
We bowed down very low.
His mother beckoned us because
We hardly dared to go.

At last approaching where He lay,
Wrapped up against the chill,
The question would not go away,
Would He the stars fulfill?

A mighty lord; this humble place;
They seemed to disagree,
But when I saw and touched His face,
I knew the King was He.

We heard our group approaching
And signed for them to stay.
Servants dug out without coaching
The bag brought for this day.

First, Melchior pulled from the pack
His wealth in polished gold.
He did not fear that he might lack
For he was very old.

Young Casper from the bundle took
A crimson leather purse
Of blended incense which he shook
To watch the dust disperse.

And I who write this, Balthazar,
Had felt compelled to bring
A jar of precious myrrh this far,
An odd gift for a king.

But, having firmly grasped the urn,
I signaled to both men
That with our gifts we should return
To honor Him again.

Before the Great King's simple throne,
We knelt and we bestowed.
Our gifts on Him, as peace unknown
Like living waters flowed.

His gentle parents were most kind
And asked if we would stay,
To rest a bit from leagues behind,
Until another day.

That night brought us a troubling dream,
Its message dark and grim
Regarding Herod's bloody scheme;
We could not go to him.

Instead, we chose another way
And hurried from that land,
Discussing all we saw that day
That we might understand.

PEACE

Peace breathes softly in the night, while
Earnest shepherds, silent, stand,
Awash in light from heaven's smile,
Commending Him Who without guile,
Elicits peace throughout the land.

Christmas Questions

The lights and colors catch my eye—
A Christmas tree stretched to the sky.
Beneath and all around it lie
Such heaps of bright, wrapped gifts that I
Must stop and ask the question, "Why
Is so much here when thousands die
For what they lack the coin to buy?"

I scan the table set for me,
Arranged, adorned so merrily;
I am amazed at what I see:
The platters heaped impressively,
Rich foods from sea to shining sea.
But, I wonder, "How can this be,
When children huddle hungrily?"

We celebrate the birth of One
Whom we believe to be God's Son.
 The cave had room, the inns had none
So, in that cave where vermin run
Was His earthly walk begun
With those for whom life was hard-won.
Did He not come for everyone?
And bear great love for those we shun,
The poor, the weak, the little one?

More questions, now, for me, for you:
Has our Christmas focus grown askew?
What is it that we ought to do?
Does Jesus' birth give us our cue?
Should we seek simplicity, too?
Ought we include some others who
Are clearly not as well-to-do?

These questions, they disturb my mind.
Perhaps, it is because I find
That I have been a little blind
To those who find life not as kind;
I am not the me my hopes defined.
A last question: am I resigned
To leave conditions as aligned—
Or with the poor to be entwined?

God Sent

To a beaten, broken land,
> God sent a quiet carpenter.

To a people under oppression,
> God sent a mourning mother.

To a world afflicted by violence and war,
> God sent an innocent infant.

To those consumed by accumulated clutter,
> God sent sheep and simple shepherds.

To those He blessed most abundantly,
> God sent three generous gentlemen.

To a race requiring redemption,
> God sent One
> born of a woman and nurtured by a man,
> who would give of Himself
> simply like a shepherd
> and extravagantly like three with no
> further need:
> His Son, Jesus the Christ.

Led by the light of His heavenly beacon,
> God sends us,
> Singing with angelic abandon,
> To welcome His Son.

Gifts: A Counter Cultural Christmas Card

Please be advised and be on guard:
The verses on this Christmas card,
Much like a shattered window's shard,
May strike you as too sharp, too hard.
But, cause exists to ill-regard
This season that our gifts have marred.

Too many gifts hurt and destroy
As did the horse received by Troy,
That only served the Grecian ploy.
Still more are kept from girl or boy,
Who, sick and starving, needs no toy,
But a gift of hope would bring great joy.

She weakly brushes flies away.
How will she make it through the day?
Does God not look down with dismay,
To see in fine words used to pray,
A faith not focused on a way
To light the lamps where life is gray?

Some children rise before the sun.
For others Christmas is not fun;
Into his arms they thrust a gun,
And so, the process has begun,
Corruption of some mother's son.
Hear their cries! Then, stay or run?

It is not only children who
Are handed gifts they quickly rue.
She demonstrates for what is true;
Her gifts are colored black and blue.
The peacemaker receives gifts, too:
Bars on the window he looks through.

With gifts, we play "The Keep Up Game."
Red Gs should mark our brows with shame
Because we image God the same
As fires are modeled by each flame,
The well-meant gift can also maim,
But has a hidden light God can reclaim.

To rectify things, Jesus came,
The Son of God, like us became.
While conditions of Christ's birth were hard,
His parents held this Gift with joy,
Who later taught and showed the way,
Then bore alone for everyone,
The penalty our sins were due,
And death's fierce grip He overcame
To the glory of God's Name.

The Tree He Would Never Forget

    The day my adventure began was as glorious as the adventure itself. The previous evening's dark skies had left a comforting white blanket on our branches. In relaxed contentment, we wafted rich clouds of aromatic scent throughout our field and beyond. Life was very good.

    People must have thought so, also. Our field was teeming with them that morning. Some of the smaller ones slapped at my branches, causing snow to shower their boots. I would have preferred that they leave my snow alone, but, their laughter at the cascading snow fit the festive mood that permeated the day.

    The sun was poised to slide into the western horizon when a small boy pointed at me and called out excitedly, "I want this one!"

"That tree is kind of crooked, Rick," his father said. "Let's look around and see if we can find one that you like even better."

"Dad, this is the one."

"We'll see. We're going to look around a little. If we don't find one we like better, we can come back for this tree. Now, let's catch up to Soriya and your mom."

As the boy turned to follow his sister and parents, he looked over his shoulder at me and smiled. "Don't worry. We'll be back."

A short while later, the family came back up the row. Rick was prancing and dancing around the other members of his family. His eyes glittered wetly. He pointed and called out, "There it is! There's my tree. Do ya see it? It's the best tree anywhere. Come on, hurry up. Let's bring it home."

Bring it home? What did that mean? I soon found out. The next thing I knew, the man was down on the snow crawling under my branches. I felt a scratch on my bark, then pain.

It was like the pain of pruning, only immeasurably worse. How can words describe torment like that? I drew within myself and tried to shut out the searing agony. I remember toppling over, separated from my roots, but it is like a dream, a nightmare. I heard the people cheering and wondered how anyone could be happy over such a catastrophe.

The man grabbed my bare stump and began to pull me over the snow. The boy gently held one of my branches and walked in his father's wake. I found a strange comfort in the boy's mittoned hand.

As they dragged me down the row, I noticed some gaps between trees. I shuttered at the thought that there was now a gap like this for me.

When we reached their vehicle, the man rolled me onto its top and tied me down securely. Soon, I was racing along. It felt like a storm except that it rushed up my trunk, wind tearing at my needles. The gale quickly ripped away what remained of my snow.

We stopped several times, but just as I began to relax, thinking my ordeal was coming to an end, we resumed our journey to ... to where, I wondered through the ache.

We finally drove into a driveway next to a small tan house. There, I was unbound and rolled from the top of the car. The woman took the children inside while the man fussed over me. He plucked at leaves that had blown into my branches and snipped away dead twigs.

He brought out a large plastic tree stand, designed to let me stand upright again. He tried to push it onto or over my stump, but it banged into some of my lower limbs. Out came a pruning saw and they were removed. "No more!" I thought. There was more. The stand did not fit and another two limbs were cut off. At last, the man was satisfied and took it into the house.

When he returned, he rolled me into a sheet and dragged me into a bright, open room in the house. The stand was there, waiting for me.

Again, the man unbound me. I was set into the stand, lifted, turned, eased back down—two or three times—until the woman said, "There. Just right." Then, while the man held me in place, she crawled under my branches and screwed bolts into my trunk. More pain.

But things improved after that. Under their mother's careful direction, the children took turns pouring glasses of water into the stand. The water was very soothing. I had not realized how thirsty I was. I began to regain my orientation now that I was vertical again. Yes, things were looking better.

"Let's decorate it," Rick shouted.

"We have to wait until the tree warms up," his father said. "Its branches are still frozen."

"I'll vacuum up the needles on the floor," his mother added, "and then you can help me spread the Christmas tree skirt. We will do the rest of the decorating tomorrow after breakfast."

When the red circular skirt had been spread out and smoothed, I was left alone. I could hear the family elsewhere in the house, but the sounds were distant and it was peaceful.

I drank deeply from the stand. Comforted by the water and the warmth of the house, I began to release my scent into the air.

I slept for several hours, then awoke to hear the mother say, "Okay, kids, it's bedtime."

"Can I say good night to the tree, first?" Rick asked.

"Yes, but don't be long."

I heard his running feet. The light came on and he was there. He just stood, looking at me.

"Come on, Rick," I heard his mother call out.

Rick inhaled a large breath of air, taking in the rich scent. He approached, gently took hold of one of my branches and rubbed it against his cheek. "Good night, Tree," he whispered. Then, he was off.

The next morning was filled with happy activity. Finding that the stand was nearly dry, the children again took turns pouring glasses of water into it. Christmas music was playing on the radio, occasionally reinforced by a voice or two from the family.

The children talked excitedly as they ate their breakfast. While the breakfast dishes were cleaned up, the man brought three boxes and set them on the floor in front of me.

He opened the first box. It contained neatly wound electrical cords with small lights along their length. He took out each loop in turn, plugged it in, and checked for any unlit bulbs.

As he did this, the children excitedly pulled baubles of various shapes and sizes from the second box. They chattered about all of them, laughed at some, and brought others to show their father. Then each was placed on the couch that sat across the room from me.

When the man finished his task, having replaced a few bulbs that had burned out, he pronounced the lights ready. The children cheered and left their baubles. Standing on a chair, the man started to arrange the electrical cords. The children took turns holding the loose end of the strings of lights as their father draped them loosely over my branches.

When they had hung the last of the lights, the man called his wife to join them. She came into the room and held his hand. He stooped down. "Ready?" he called out. "One, two, three!"

I was suddenly aglow with color. The children shouted in unison, "Hooray!"

The family was not yet done with me. The children went back and forth between the couch and me, selecting their favorite baubles and placing them on branches they could reach. Their parents decorated higher up. One lower branch, facing the couch, was left bare, as was my pointy top branch.

When the couch was clear, they opened the third box. "Be careful, kids. Go slowly," their mother told the children.

The members of the family took turns removing and carefully unwrapping a set of neatly painted plaster figurines, placing each piece gently on the couch. At the bottom of the box was a board on which someone had constructed what looked like a shed with one of the walls missing. They placed it under my bare lower branch.

The children arranged the figures in and around the shed. In the shed were a donkey, a woman in blue, a man in brown, and a trough containing hay with an indentation in the center. Outside the shed, there were four sheep and three men in gray, one of them carrying a lamb. All the figures appeared to be looking at the trough.

The woman placed a final plaster figure, a large white star, near the end of the bare branch. It hung right above the building.

The man retrieved the chair. After he had stepped up on it, his wife handed him a lacy white angel, which he carefully set over my pointy top branch. Again, the children cheered.

Together, the family picked up the cloths they had removed from the figures, put them back in their box and removed the boxes from the room.

The area around me now clear, the family sat down on the couch and silently looked at me. The man finally spoke. "You were right about the tree, Rick. It's a beaut."

Rick flashed a big smile and cuddled under his father's arm.

Each day thereafter, Rick visited me and checked my water. Sometimes, he brought his sister, leading her by the hand. He would gently hold the ornaments within his reach, often humming or singing Christmas songs as he did so. He would rearrange the plaster figures and, if Soriya was with him, Rick would tell her about Baby Jesus.

On one visit, Rick and Soriya brought three brightly colored packages. They crawled underneath me to place them against my trunk. Occasionally, one of the parents, too, would slip in and add to the small clusters of brightly wrapped packages.

Before leaving, he never failed to caress my branches, smelling my scent and savoring the prickle of my needles against the skin of his hands. He would tell me how beautiful I was and say that I was "The best tree ever."

The first pink rays of the sun had scarcely touched the eastern sky when I heard the patter of running feet in the hallway. They became muffled thumps as they reached the carpet of the living room. When the footsteps stopped, Rick was there.

He stood, muscles taut and body quivering in excitement as he beheld the packages that surrounded me. He seemed to recover himself slightly and then broke into excited shouts, "It's Christmas! Wow! It's Christmas!"

Like a magnet, this brought out Soriya, who scampered over to touch the vision that held her brother enthralled. Their mother was not far behind, quietly saying, "Merry Christmas, kids," as she scooped them into a big hug. She kissed each of them on the cheek and added, "Go cuddle up with Daddy while I make breakfast. After we eat, you may open your presents."

"Yes, Mommy," Soriya said with a tinge of reluctance in her voice. She took Rick's hand and he allowed himself to be led from the room, looking back over his shoulder as he walked.

"Hop in," I heard their father's voice call out.
He may have been hoping that they would doze off, allowing him to do the same. He had worked well into

the morning on the floor in front of me. Parts scattered all around him, he had assembled the bicycle that now leaned against the wall behind me.

After winding rolls of paper around the bike, he positioned it and other presents beneath me, trying to give the illusion that they were more plentiful than they really were. He was careful to leave an open area around the wooden structure.

It was not long before the pajama-clad family gathered in front of me. It had taken little time to prepare breakfast. It had taken less time to eat it. The man had plugged in my lights and, from the glow in their faces, I was sure that my glory rivaled the sun's.

"May we open presents, now?" Rick's voice piped up, interrupting the reverie of the others.

"In a minute, Rick," his father said. "We can't forget the most important gift of all."

Rick's mother handed him the small plaster figure of an infant. "Here you go, dear, place Baby Jesus in the manger."

Rick gazed at the figure cupped in his hands. He looked up at me and then turned to his sister, "Soriya may do it. I got to pick the tree."

The other three members of the family held hands as they watched Soriya gently fit the infant onto the trough. She took her mother's outstretched hand and listened to her father say simply, "Father in heaven, thank you for the most precious gift of your Son."

They all said, "Amen." The children followed their response with an expectant look at their father.

He smiled and said, "Go to it...but one at a time, Rick." With a twinkle in his eye, he added, "And make sure that it is your present before you open it."

Rick dove for the large package, the wrapping of which did little to disguise the bicycle inside. He read his name, then sent streamers and scraps of paper flying everywhere.

Soriya recognized her name on one of the presents. She pulled it out from underneath me and set to stripping off its silvery wrapping. She was less frantic than her brother, but every bit as efficient. It did not take her long to set free the stuffed, brown and white kitten within.

Following Rick's example, Soriya brought the kitten to the couch, where their parents sat, sipping coffee and watching the pair of tornadoes touching down here and there around me.

As the number of wrapped gifts dwindled, Soriya slid from the couch, and took several dancing steps around me. When she came to her brother, she tapped his arm and asked, "Can we give the presents now?"

Rick had been bent over an oversized stocking, studying each small treasure as he removed it. At Soriya's question, Rick hesitated. The stocking still had treasures for him to mine from its depths.

Suddenly, he grinned. "I bet I can find them first," he called as he dove under my boughs and swam through a sea of torn wrapping paper to my trunk.

The presents were not where they had put them. "Hey!" he called out and, forgetting where he was, he tried to stand up.

I began to tip over, but the father had anticipated trouble and quickly grabbed me. "Whoa, Rick. Easy, now."

All were relieved when, once again, I was securely vertical.

Soriya had already retrieved the gifts from the debris. The children gave them to their parents and soon I was wearing two bright new ornaments. I was proud of the two wreaths, one encircling the smiling face of each child.

The floor was littered with clothes, art supplies, a few toys, and wrapping paper, lots of wrapping paper. The family stuffed paper into billowing trash bags and organized the gifts into two piles. Rick's was in the shadow of his first two-wheeler and Soriya's between the couch and end table.

Two small packages remained unopened under my limbs. A third was squeezed between Rick's folded arms and his chest, as he watched the rest of his family leave the room.

When they were gone, Rick sat next to me and gently caressed several branches before speaking. "I'm sorry that I almost knocked you over. And I'm sure glad that Dad is a good catcher."

Suddenly remembering the package in his arms, he added, "This is for you. I know you can't open it, so I'll open it for you. See? It's a picture of my family.. Here's Dad and Mom and Soriya, and this is me right next to you. I colored it myself. Do you like it?"

"Oh, yes!" I cried out in the silence. "It is beautiful." This and so much more was in my heart, but even my greatest efforts did not bring forth any more words than my limbs produced apples.

Rick crawled under me and leaned the picture against my trunk. Then, before leaving, he stood back and looked at me for a long moment. "I love you, Tree," he whispered. The words, "I love you, Rick," welled up within me.

Having begun with more-than-expected excitement, the remainder of the day was filled with happy but more reserved activity for the family.

They prepared and went to church. Upon their return, the children played quietly in front of me as their parents worked in the kitchen, all waiting for the arrival of Grandma Magee and dinner time.

When Grandma Magee arrived, I heard happy voices at the door, greeting her. After the obligatory hug, Rick grabbed her hand and tugged until she came with him to the living room. Not to see his new bicycle, but to see me. "Look at our tree, Grandma. I picked it. Isn't it the best, most beautiful tree ever?"

She crouched down, hugged her grandson, and gave him a kiss on the cheek. Down at his level, she looked into his eyes and spoke softly, emphasizing each word, "It is a wonderful tree, Rick. You did a great job picking it."

After dinner, the children opened the gifts Grandma Magee had brought. She, in turn, opened the two remaining in the shadow of my branches.

Rick gave her an ornament he had molded using homemade clay and carefully painted. "Why, it's your Christmas tree," she said. "I love it, Rick. Thank you." She nearly dropped it as Rick buried himself in her embrace.

Grandma Magee was equally effusive in her praise and thanks for Soriya's gift, a Christmas wreath pin. Careful of Soriya who was cuddled in her lap, she immediately pinned it on her dress, heedless of the holes it made in the silky fabric.

That night, before going to bed, Rick came to visit. He knelt down and caressed each of the plaster figures in turn. He gazed up at me, kissed the branch from which the star hung, got up and left, all without saying a word.

Rick continued to visit me at various times—in the morning when he awoke, during the day, in the evening. Sometimes he was animated and at other times, quiet. It was as if, even at six years of age, Rick recognized that everything was shadow after the glory of that great exciting day.

Meanwhile, each dawn found my branches more bare, as I littered the tree skirt with needles. One day, I lost more than dried needles. The family wrapped the stable with its figures, and returned them to their box. Likewise, ornaments and strings of lights were returned to their respective boxes.

Finally, with Rick crying softly at my side, I was dragged from the house. I am on a plowed up bank of snow at the edge of the street. Soon, I will be hauled even further away from this house and from Rick.

Despite my condition, when Rick comes outside, he runs over the snow to me. He gently brushes away my dead needles and whispers, "You were the best tree. Ever."

In the final moments before my last spark becomes a lifeless coal, I reflect back on the past few weeks. I delight in the lights and glory. Yet, it was not glory, but love—love that gave meaning, first, to my pain, and then to my splendor. Now, though the splendor is gone, love remains; though life pass away, the love lives on.

The Gift of Writing

You cannot know the number of pages remaining in your heavenly ledger. How long do you have to voice the words He has given you to speak?

In view of this uncertainty, it would behoove us to take advantage of opportunities that present themselves. Hence these closing thoughts.

The Creator, God of infinite generosity, saw fit to bestow on me a feel for words. This ability to manipulate and organize words on paper, the gift of writing, has been a source of much joy and wonder. I greatly prize this gift and am passionate about its use.

The film, *Chariots of Fire*, chronicles the efforts of British runners to prepare for and compete in the 1924 Olympic Games. One of the central figures in the film is Scottish runner Eric Liddell, the son of missionary parents.

In one scene, his sister pleads ardently for Eric to put aside the triviality of competitive running and return to the mission field in China. Liddell responds, "[God] also made me fast. And when I run, I feel His pleasure."

He felt God's pleasure in his use of the gift. Is there not always pleasure in the appropriate use of God's gifts?

I cannot answer this question with certainty, but my gut feeling is that it ought to be true. I know that I delight in exercising the gift of writing. I feel a participation in the ongoing creative work of God. With it, I assemble words to produce an original poem, one that has never before been read or heard. Pretty heady stuff.

As with any gift, there is the excitement of anticipation as I continue to unwrap it. Occasionally, I catch a glimpse of what it might look like in a mature state, fully unwrapped.

I read a poem that astonishes me. I sit back, reread it and whisper in wonder to myself, "Where did that come from? It is too good to be mine." This collection contains some poems of this caliber. I leave it to you to go back and find them.

Finally, I cannot deny that positive or, at least, thoughtful responses of readers pleases me. It is rewarding when someone rereads a poem, laughs at a passage or wipes away a tear after reading something I have written. It is both intoxicating and humbling to think that God has used my writing to touch another person's life.

This raises questions regarding misuse and responsible use of the gift. These are important issues, but they will wait for another book and another epilogue. For now, I intend to thank God for the gift of writing and then to savor all that is *The Joy and Wonder of Christmas*.

Sharing the Joy and Wonder of Christmas

When an experience touches us, our natural inclination is to share that experience. So, I invite you to share an experience of Christmas with a friend or family member, ... and then allow yourself to become engaged as she shares her Christmas story with you.

Finally, if you would like to share this Christmas memory with me, I would be delighted to hear from you. You may reach me at the following address: JoyAndWonder@TheMaineSeasons.com

www.ingramcontent.com/pod-product-compliance
Lightning Source LLC
Chambersburg PA
CBHW071302040426
42444CB00009B/1841